CONTENTS

WORDS THAT LOOK LIKE THIS CAN BE FOUND IN THE GLOSSARY ON PAGE 24.

GALAPAGOS PENGUINS

ROCKHOPPER PENGUIN

EMPEROR PENGUIN

ADÉLIE PENGUIN

Penguins are a type of flightless bird. They live in lots of different places. Penguins are known for their strong flippers and wobbly waddle. There are 18 species of penguin in the world.

Perfect PENGUINS

GALAPAGOS PENGUIN

Written by Bethany Latham

Enslow PUBLISHING

Published in 2026 by Enslow Publishing, LLC
2544 Clinton Street
Buffalo, NY 14224

Written by: Bethany Latham
Edited by: Rebecca Phillips-Bartlett
Designed by: Amy Li

Cataloging-in-Publication Data

Names: Latham, Bethany, author.
Title: Galapagos penguin / Bethany Latham.
Description: Buffalo, NY : Enslow Publishing, 2026. | Series: Perfect penguins | Includes glossary and index.
Identifiers: ISBN 9781978547407 (pbk.) | ISBN 9781978547414 (library bound) | ISBN 9781978547421 (ebook)
Subjects: LCSH: Galapagos penguin--Juvenile literature.
Classification: LCC QL696.S473 L834 2026 | DDC 598.47--dc23

Manufactured in the United States of America

CPSIA compliance information: Batch #QW26ENS: For further information contact Enslow Publishing LLC, New York, New York at 1-800-398-2504.

Please visit our website, www.enslowpublishing.com. For a free color catalog of all our high-quality books, call toll free 1-800-398-2504 or fax 1-877-980-4454.

Find us on

IMAGE CREDITS

All images are courtesy of Shutterstock.com, unless otherwise stated.

Recurring – Martyshova Maria (doodles and arrows). Cover – Photos by Guy, Dominyk Lever. 2–3 – Steve Allen. 4–5 – Risto Raunio, Goldilock Project, Kareen Broodryk, William2023. 6–7 – aarbois, Lauren Squire. 8–9 – Maridav, Ps-Fotos. 10–11 – Watch The World. 12–13 – Sydni Josowitz, Steve Allen. 14–15 – aviben, asiadomaga. 16–17 – NatashaFa, Don Mammoser, Nina B. 18–19 – Danita Delimont, Alex Vog, Photos by Guy. 20–21 – wildestanimal, Maksim Safaniuk. 22–23 – nodrama_llama, Ben Queenborough.

Galapagos penguins are one of the world's smallest penguins. They grow to be around 20 inches (50 cm) tall. Galapagos penguins live farther north than any other species of penguin.

HABITAT

Galapagos penguins are only found in the Galapagos Islands. These are near the country of Ecuador, which is in South America. Galapagos penguins live on the western islands. These islands have cold water currents that carry the fish they eat.

An animal's natural home is called its habitat.

The Galapagos Islands are made of rock that came from volcanoes. Galapagos penguins make their homes in caves and crevasses in the rock. Crevasses are big cracks in the rocks.

BODY

Galapagos penguins have black and white feathers. The white feathers on their heads make a C-shape. The Galapagos Islands are very hot. Galapagos penguins have lots of ways of keeping their bodies cool.

Galapagos penguins do not have feathers around their eyes, cheeks, or beaks. This helps them stay cool. They stand with their flippers out and bend over their feet to keep them in shadow.

Like dogs, Galapagos penguins pant to keep cool.

GETTING AROUND

Galapagos penguins are fast swimmers. They can swim up to 22 miles (35 km) an hour. Galapagos penguins are good divers. Their dives are often short and shallow. However, they can dive over 88 feet (27 m) deep.

During the day, when it is very hot, Galapagos penguins go into the ocean. They sleep on the beach at night. Galapagos penguins do not travel very far. They often stay close to the islands.

LIFE CYCLE

A life cycle is the stages of an animal's life that lead to the animal having their own young.

Most penguins only mate at a certain time of year. However, Galapagos penguins mate all year round. They are the only species of penguin to do this.

Galapagos penguins have one mate for their whole lives. Mates clean each other's feathers and tap their beaks together. They build nests in cracks in the rock. Nests are made of sticks, leaves, and feathers.

YOUNG GALAPAGOS PENGUIN

The female penguin lays up to two eggs. Both parents take turns looking after the eggs. The eggs hatch after about 38 days. The mother and father both feed the chicks for the first 30 days.

Galapagos penguin chicks have fluffy brown or gray feathers. They leave the nest after about 60 days. After three to six months, young penguins can look after themselves. They can have young after three years.

FAMILY LIFE

Galapagos penguins are social animals. They live in groups called colonies. Galapagos penguin colonies are often smaller than other penguin colonies. Penguins often build their nests away from others to find shade and keep cool.

Galapagos penguins try to keep each other safe from predators. They call and flap their flippers to warn each other and scare the predators away.

DIET AND DANGERS

Galapagos penguins eat cold-water fish, such as sardines and anchovies. They often hunt alone or in small groups. The penguins dive down underneath the fish, then swim upwards to catch them.

A diet is the type of food an animal eats.

In the ocean, Galapagos penguins are in danger of being eaten by sharks, fur seals, and sea lions. Penguins also face danger from cats, dogs, and rats. These animals steal eggs and eat the penguins.

PROTECT THE PENGUINS

Galapagos penguins are endangered. This means they are at risk of dying out. The oceans are warming up. This is affecting cold-water fish and leaving the penguins without food.

Galapagos penguins are the rarest type of penguin in the world.

Oil spills and plastic pollution also affect Galapagos penguins. However, people are trying to protect the penguins. The Galapagos Islands are looked after by people. Some scientists are making nests to help the penguins.

Plastic pollution includes plastic bottles, bags, food wrappers and more.

PERFECT PENGUINS

Galapagos penguins are very clever birds. We have seen all the ways that they are perfectly suited to living in their hot habitat. How do you keep cool in warm weather?

A home without pollution is very important. How could you help stop pollution to protect the penguins?

What was your favorite Galapagos penguin fact? Would you like to meet a Galapagos penguin?

GLOSSARY

CURRENTS	continuous movements of a body of water in a particular direction
MATE	to produce young with an animal of the same species
OIL SPILLS	when oil leaks into the sea or other types of water, such as a lake
POLLUTION	harmful and poisonous things being added to an environment
PREDATORS	animals that hunt other animals for food
SHALLOW	not very deep
SOCIAL	to do with being in a group or community
SPECIES	a group of very similar animals or plants that can create young together
VOLCANOES	large mountains that have hot, melted rock inside

INDEX